This book belongs to

50

Coloring page.

Printed on single-sided paper.

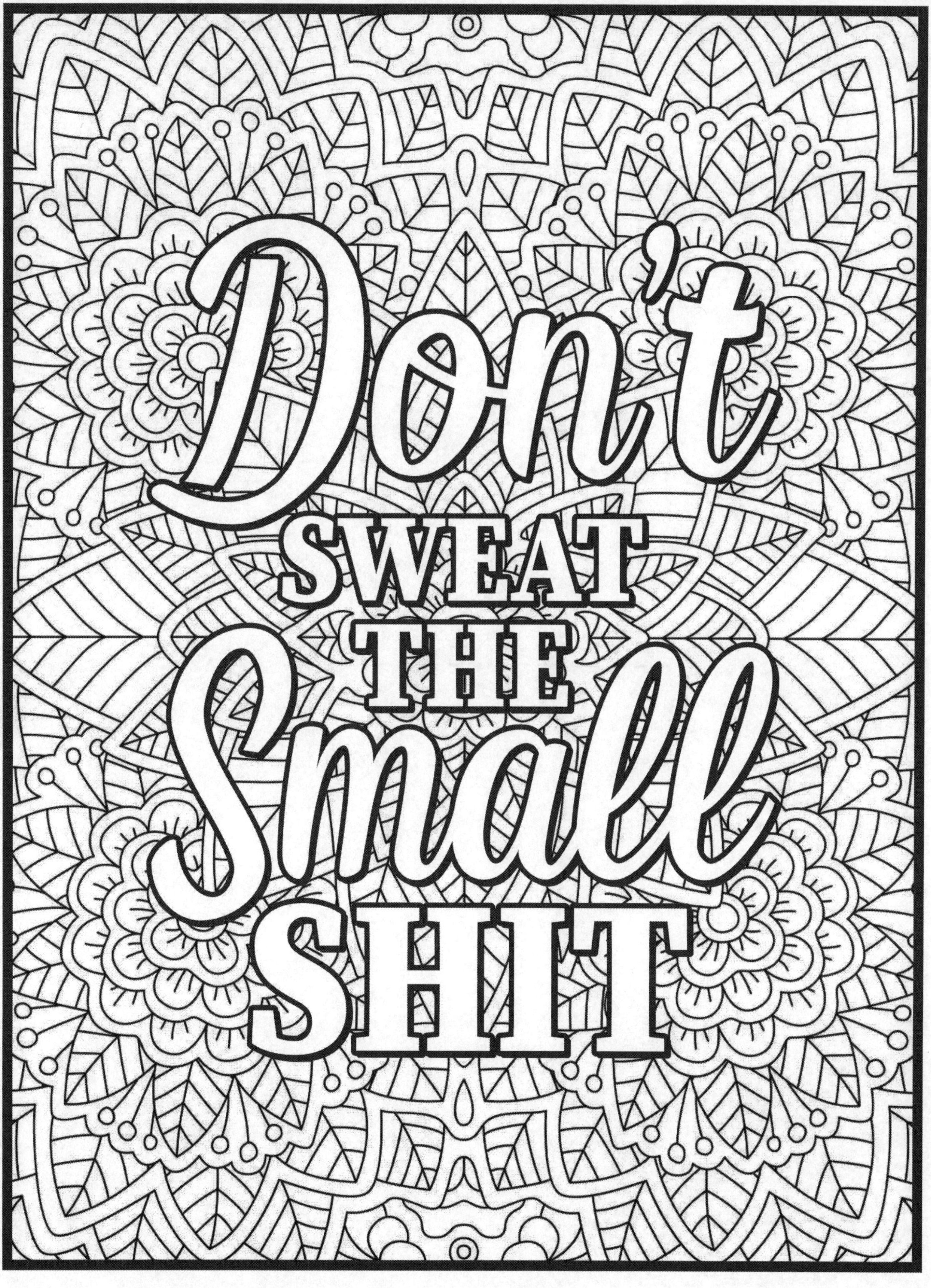
Don't
SWEAT
THE
Small
SHIT

I CAN
And I
FUCKING
Will

Go
WITH THE
fucking
FLOW

You are
amazing
as
Fuck

GOEST
AND
FUCKETH
THYSELF

HUSTLE
Your
ASS OFF
Mofo!

You
ARE THE
SHIT!

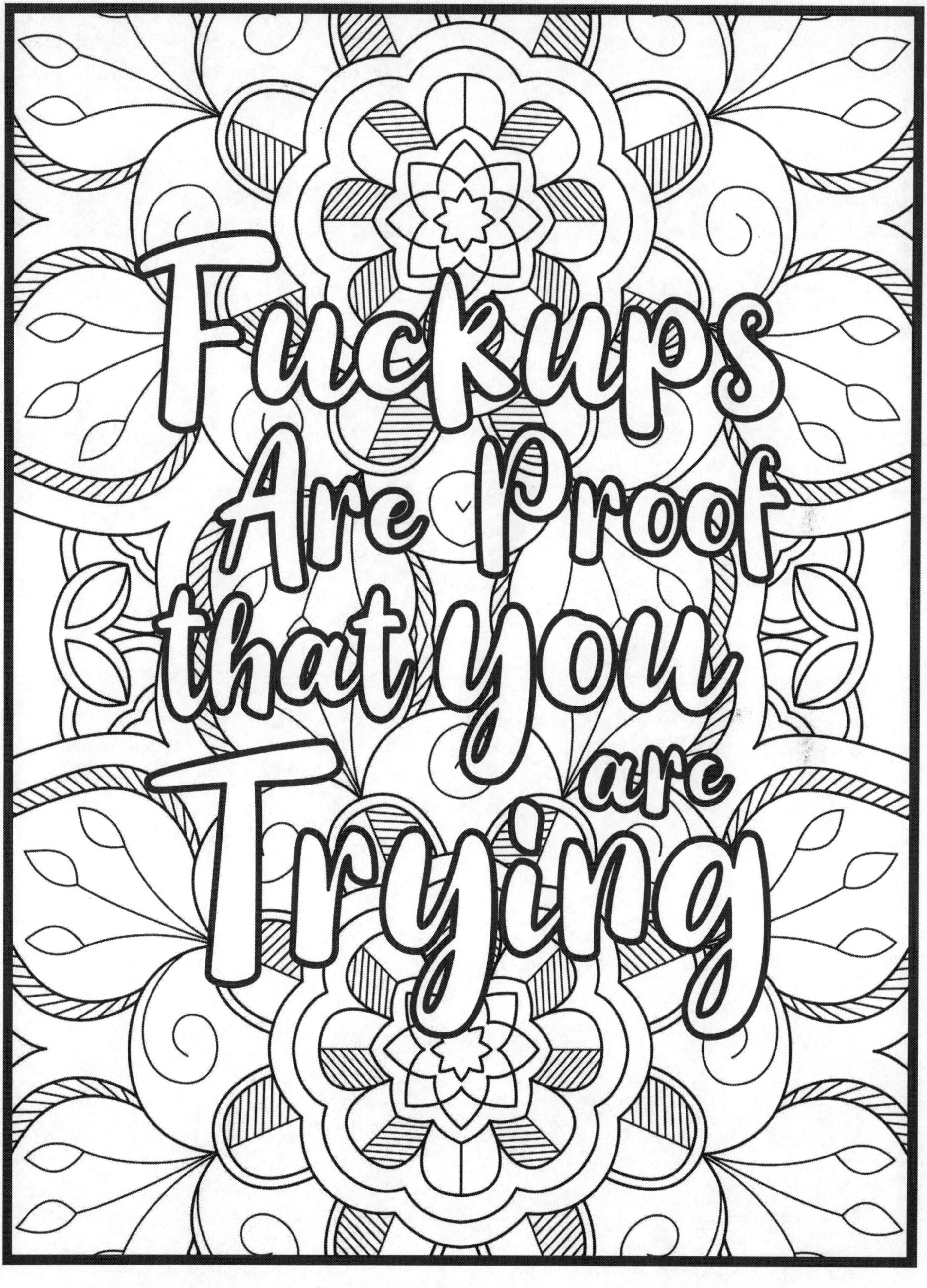
Fuckups
Are Proof
that you
are
Trying

BE HAPPY.
IT DRIVES
ASSHOLES
CRAZY.

WAKE UP.
Kick Some
FUCKING
ass
REPEAT

You are
AWESOME
as fuck

Smile More
WORRY
Fucking
less.

You
FUCKING
Got
THIS.

Slay
ALL
MOTHERFUCKING
Day!

ONCE IN A
WHiLE
BLOW
YOUR OWN
DAMN MiND

Rise
and
Grind
Motherfuckers!

inhale
THE GOOD SHIT
exhale
THE BULLSHIT

When it
Rains,
LOOK FOR THE
Fucking
RAINBOWS

let's
FUCK
shit up

GET
SHIT
DONE

be the
BEST
fuck the
REST

FUCK
HATERS

Namaste
MOTHERFUCKERS!

CHILL
#THE
F*CK
OUT

BREAK THE
Fucking
RULES

FUCK
PANDEMIC

Never
Fucking
Give Up!

FUCK
That
SHIT

Your Fuckups Don't Define You

Be Happy
EVERY
Damn
DAY

AND SHE
GAVE ZERO
FUCKS.
NOT EVEN
ONE.
SHE LIVED
HAPPILY
EVER AFTER.
THE, END.

Take
NO SHIT
Give
NO FUCKS

OVERCOME
ALL THE SHIT
THAT WAS
MEANT TO
DESTROY
YOU

I wish i was
A UNICORN
so i could stab
ASSHOLES
with my HORN

I AM
KIND OF
A BIG
FUCKING
DEAL

FUCK
FUCKER

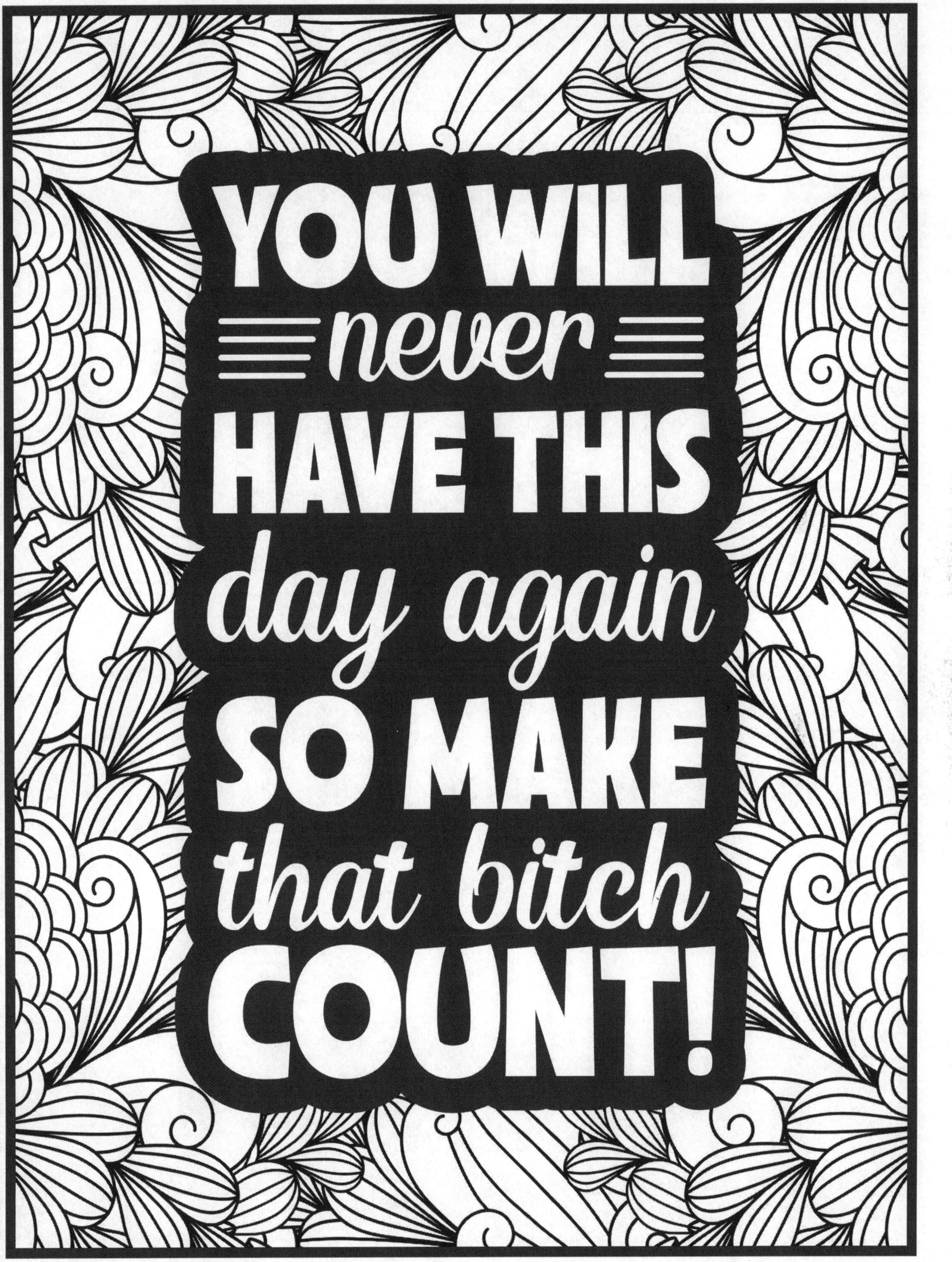
YOU WILL
never
HAVE THIS
day again
SO MAKE
that bitch
COUNT!

ZERO
FUCK

CHEER
the
FUCK UP

DO THE
FUCKING
IMPOSSIBLE

YOU ARE
FUCKING
ADORABLE

Do epic
SHIT

Bloom wherever
THE FUCK
You are
PLANTED

BITCH
SLAP
YOUR
STRESS

Make it
FUCKING
Happen

I MAKE
This Shit
LOOK EASY

FUCK OFF
Bitch

DON'T BE
A LADY
Be a
FUCKING
LEGEND.

Carpe
THAT
Fucking
DIEM

SPREAD
love
EVERYWHERE
you
FUCKING
GO

Manufactured by Amazon.ca
Bolton, ON

42459080R00057